Simple Money Rituals

Money Magick For Wealth and Success

By Eyvette Risher

Printed in the United States of America
ISBN: 979-8-9899172-5-9
First Printing, April 2025

Cover & Interior Design by: Eyvette Risher

Published by:
My World of Metaphysics LLC
Eyvette Risher
New York
www.myworldofmetaphysics.com

Table of Contents

Table of Contents

Rituals

Completion

About the Author

Eyvette Risher is the creator and owner of My World of Metaphysics LLC, a platform dedicated to empowering individuals through spirituality, manifestation rituals, angel work, and metaphysical teachings. As a metaphysical life coach, Eyvette specializes in guiding others to harness their inner power and transform their lives through practical rituals and spiritual insights.

With a passion for spreading New Age wisdom, Eyvette is best known for her engaging content on YouTube and social media, where she shares practical tools for manifesting abundance, love, protection, and spiritual growth. She is also the proud owner of an online metaphysical boutique that serves as a sanctuary for those seeking ritual supplies.

Eyvette's mission is to inspire and uplift others, providing them with the knowledge and practices needed to create a life filled with purpose, prosperity, and peace.

Dedication

This book is dedicated to my family, friends, and the many authors whose books have guided me over the decades.
To my loyal YouTube followers—thank you for supporting me and standing by me on this journey. You've been my rock in ways you may never realize.

To my assistant in the creation of this book—you helped make this vision real.

Most importantly, to my mother, Shellie—your love and courage gave me the strength to pursue my dreams and stay true to who I am. Without you, I don't know who or where I would be.

Thank you. I love you.
– Eyvette

What to Expect in This Book

Although this book is titled "Everyday Money Rituals," it's about so much more than just money. It's a book filled with simple rituals for creating success, prosperity, opportunities and yes, bringing you closer to your money dreams. Whether you're looking to attract financial freedom, secure a new home, purchase a car, land a career promotion, start a business, or simply bring more abundance into your life, this book provides the tools to help you manifest it.

Inside, you'll find a collection of simple, powerful rituals designed to align your energy with the frequency of wealth and success. Using everyday tools like herbs, candles, crystals, scripting and more, you'll learn how to work with the Universe to bring your desires into reality. These rituals are not just about attracting money—they're about unlocking the door to a life of opportunity, stability, and freedom.

This book is your guide to stepping into your power and co-creating the life you deserve. Whether you're new to rituals and manifesting or experienced, get ready to take your manifestations to the next level.

Powerful "Fehu" Rune Symbol for Money

The Fehu rune (ᚠ) is an ancient symbol of wealth, abundance, and prosperity. Its energy is rooted in the concept of material gain, financial success, and the flow of resources.

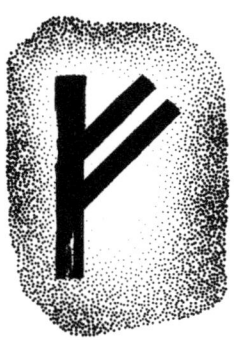

By focusing on this symbol, you can align yourself with the frequency of abundance and activate the flow of wealth into your life.

Why It's Used in This Book:

This rune serves as a powerful tool to enhance the rituals in this book, anchoring your intentions and amplifying it's effects. As you work with the rituals, let the energy of the Fehu rune sign guide you toward financial prosperity and opportunities.

The Real Magic Behind Money Magick

Let me tell you something: the real magic isn't in the herbs, the candles, or the crystals. Those are tools, and yes, they're powerful when used the right way—but the real magic is in YOU. It's in your belief, your faith, and your determination to move forward, even when the odds feel stacked against you. Trust me, I'm speaking from experience.

Belief and Faith: My Journey

- I wasn't the smartest person growing up. I was in speech class, struggling to keep up at times, but let me tell you what I did have: belief. I always believed in myself, even when other people doubted me or when things didn't come easy. I wasn't a genius, but I had the courage to move forward no matter what.
- By 16, I graduated high school. I didn't just stop there. I pushed forward, got my business degree, and later became a nurse. I didn't just work as a nurse—I kept climbing. I got my bachelor's degree, then my master's degree. And then, I went on to own a 12-unit apartment building. All of this didn't happen because I was lucky or because someone handed me anything.

It happened because I believed in myself and knew that there was a power inside me—a divine power—working through me.

This belief didn't just help me survive; it helped me thrive. When you believe, you open doors that you didn't even know existed. You send out a signal to the Universe saying, "I'm ready, let's go!" And the Universe will meet you halfway, every time.

Clarity of Desire: Know What You Want

One thing I've learned is that you have to be clear about what you want. The Universe isn't going to guess for you. Back when I decided I wanted to own property, I didn't just say, "I want to own something." No, I said, "I want to own a multi-unit apartment building, and I want to create something that will generate wealth for me and my family." I got specific, and guess what? That's exactly what happened.

When you know what you want, it's like drawing a map for the Universe. The more clear and detailed you are, the faster you'll see results. If I could go from speech class to owning an apartment building, trust me, you can do it too. The key is to see it, believe it, and speak it into existence.

Action: Belief Without Action is Nothing

Let me be real with you—belief is powerful, but it doesn't work without action. You can light all the candles and burn all the bay leaves you want, but if you're not putting in the work, it's not going to happen. When I wanted to go back to school, I didn't just sit around hoping it would happen. I enrolled, studied, and sacrificed time to make it work. When I wanted to own property, I didn't wait for someone to give it to me —I did the research, saved my money, and made the moves. That's what action looks like.

Rituals help focus your energy and set your intentions, but you have to meet the Universe halfway. Show the Universe you're serious, and it will move mountains for you.

The Power Working Through You

I believe with my whole heart that everything comes from the Universe—or God, or whatever you call your higher power. Remember there is only one with many names.

That divine force is what's working through you in every ritual, every prayer, and every step you take. When you trust that this power is on your side, you become unstoppable.

Let me break it down: the Universe wants you to win. It's not out there trying to block your blessings. It's waiting for you to align your energy, get clear about your desires, and take action. That's when the magic happens—not just because of the ritual, but because of the power that's already inside of you.

Your Inner Power

If there's one thing I want you to take from this, it's this: you have the power. The rituals are tools, but the magic comes from YOU. When you believe in yourself, trust the process, and take action, you unlock something unstoppable.

I've been where you are—dreaming of something better, wondering if it's even possible. I'm here to tell you it is. I'm proof of it. If I could do it, so can you.

Much Love
Eyvette

How to Use This Book

Before jumping into the rituals, take a moment to read the basics before the rituals, these are the foundation of successful manifestation.

Understanding magical timing, colors, and setting intentions will help amplify your results. This book is designed to be a blueprint, not a rulebook. Use these rituals as a starting point, but don't be afraid to get creative and have fun.

You can jump right to the section that fits your needs or read the book in order—there's no wrong way to use it.

But most importantly—stay open, trust the process, and have fun. The magic is already within you.

The Law of Attraction and Rituals

Before diving into rituals, it is important to understand the Law of Attraction and how it plays a crucial role in manifestation. The Law of Attraction states that like attracts like—the energy you put out into the universe is what you will receive in return.

Every thought, feeling, and belief you hold carries a vibration that attracts experiences that match that frequency.

When performing money rituals, it is not just about lighting a candle or using herbs; it is about aligning your mindset, energy, and intention with the abundance you seek.

Here's how the basics of the Law of Attraction can help with your rituals:

- Clarity – Clearly define your financial goals. The more specific you are, the easier it is to attract what you want.

- Belief – Have unwavering faith that your desires are already yours. Doubt weakens manifestations.

- Emotion – Feel the joy and excitement as if you already have the abundance you desire.

- Visualization – Regularly visualize yourself in the reality of wealth, success, and financial security.

- Action – Take inspired steps toward financial success while trusting the universe to guide you.

- Gratitude – Express thankfulness for what you have and what's on its way to you.

- Release - Here is where most mess up! You must release and let go allowing the Universe to use it's magical force. Let go of the How!

Importance of Ethical Manifestation

It is essential to perform rituals with pure intentions and for the highest good of all involved. The Law of Attraction and the Law of Karma state that the energy you send out will always return to you. Engaging in manipulative or harmful practices is never positive or in alignment for the betterment of all involved.

The rituals in this book are based on white magick and positive energy, intended only for attracting abundance, success, and opportunities in ethical and uplifting ways. Always practice with integrity, gratitude, and an open heart.

Understanding the Basics of Rituals

Before engaging in money rituals, understanding foundational spiritual and energetic principles can enhance your success. Knowing how the elements, colors, crystals, moon phases, herbs, and days of the week influence manifestation allows you to align your rituals with natural forces that support your goals.

Each ritual is not just about the physical action (lighting a candle, using herbs, etc.), but about the energy and intention behind it. When you combine the power of the Law of Attraction with the right tools and timing, you create a potent force that amplifies results.

Now, let's explore the essential components that influence money manifestation.

The Elements and Money Rituals

Understanding the elements is essential when performing money rituals, as each element carries a unique energy that can enhance your manifestations.

Here's how to use them:

- Fire – Represents transformation, passion, and action. Use candles, bonfires, or incense to energize your money rituals and speed up manifestation.

- Water – Symbolizes intuition, flow, and emotional connection. Use moon water, Florida water, or baths to cleanse financial blockages and invite prosperity.

- Air – Represents communication, clarity, and new ideas. Use incense, feathers, or written affirmations to call in new financial opportunities.

- Earth – Symbolizes stability, grounding, and material wealth. Use crystals, herbs, or bury money petitions in soil can assist you to manifest financial security.

Colors in Money Manifestation

Colors play a vital role in rituals, each carrying specific energies that enhance manifestation. When using candles, clothing, or crystals, consider these meanings:

- Green – Wealth, financial growth, abundance.
- Gold – Prosperity, success, high earnings.
- Yellow – Intuition, clarity, spiritual guidance while making decisions, and creativity.
- Red – Passion, motivation, action in achieving financial goals.
- Black – Protection, removing financial blockages, banishing debt.
- White – Purity, clarity in financial decisions, amplifies other colors.
- Brown – Earthy grounding, abundance in all forms, financial stability.
- Orange – Success, ambition, prosperity in all endeavors.
- Blue – Communication, clarity, financial negotiations, business success.

Intention Oils For Money

Use these oils in your money rituals to call in wealth and abundance. You can use them on their own or mix them to make your own money oil.

Money Oils List:
- Money Attracting Oil
- Money Drawing Oil
- Prosperity Oil
- Magnet Oil
- Attraction Oil
- High John the Conqueror Oil
- Road Opener Oil
- Better Business Oil
- Bayberry
- Lavender Oil
- Holy Oil
- Success Oil
- Helping Hand Oil
- Olive Oil (programmed for money rituals)

How to Use:
Anoint your candle, paper, or other tools noted in this book with the oil(s) of your choice.
Focus on your money wish while using the oil.
Let these oils boost your intention and help you bring money and abundance into your life.

Crystals for Wealth and Success

Crystals can amplify energy and assist in attracting wealth. Here are some powerful stones for money and success:

- Citrine – The 'merchant's stone,' attracts abundance and financial success.

- Green Aventurine – Luck, new opportunities, and financial prosperity.

- Pyrite – Also known as "Fool's Gold," brings wealth and confidence. Also used for protection of wealth.

- Clear Quartz – Enhances intentions and magnifies manifestation power.

- Amethyst – Spiritual clarity, intuition in financial decisions.

- Tiger's Eye – Encourages confidence, willpower, and prosperity.

- Black Tourmaline – Protects against financial negativity and energy blockages.

- Red Jasper – Boosts motivation and endurance for financial success.

- Jade – Attracts luck, abundance, and long-term prosperity.

These are just a few to note and have available when needed.

Moon Cycles and Money Manifestation

The moon phases influence manifestation rituals. Aligning rituals with moon cycles can enhance results:

- New Moon – Set financial intentions, begin new money ventures.

- Waxing Moon – Growth, increasing wealth, attracting opportunities.

- Full Moon – Amplifying financial success, gratitude rituals.

- Waning Moon – Releasing debt, removing financial obstacles.

Magical Herbs for Money and Success

Herbs have been used for centuries to attract wealth. Use them in baths, candles, or spells:

- Cinnamon – Speeding up success, drawing money quickly.

- Bay Leaves – Writing wishes, financial petitions, burning for manifestation.

- Basil – Prosperity, attracting financial stability.

- Mint – Success in business, fresh financial opportunities.

- Chamomile – Luck, prosperity, drawing in unexpected wealth.

- Allspice – Luck, financial success, and fast money.

- Sea Salt – Purification, removing financial blockages, protection.

- Nutmeg – Gambling luck, prosperity, and good fortune.

- Clove – Protection, attracting wealth, and clearing obstacles.

- Ginger – Speeding up manifestations, financial success.

- Star Anise – Psychic awareness, success in money matters.

- Bayberry – Wealth, prosperity, attracting abundance.

- Patchouli – Drawing money, success in business, and wealth attraction.

- Pecans: Prosperity and abundance

Days of the Week for Money Rituals

Each day has specific planetary energy that can enhance rituals:

- Monday (Moon) – Intuition, emotions, financial planning.

- Tuesday (Mars) – Action, determination, breaking financial barriers.

- Wednesday (Mercury) – Communication, contracts, business success.

- Thursday (Jupiter) – Abundance, expansion, prosperity.

- Friday (Venus) – Attracting money with ease, wealth, luxury, self-love, and love for your desired wish.

- Saturday (Saturn) – Financial discipline, clearing debts, long-term wealth, removing negativity around money, success, and abundance, and clearing energy.

- Sunday (Sun) – Success, confidence, financial strength.

Understanding these foundational elements will help you get the most out of your money rituals. When you combine the Law of Attraction with the right tools and timing, your manifestations become stronger and more aligned with your desires.

Now, let's move forward into the practice of money rituals!

Simple Money Rituals
"Money flows to me with ease and grace."

- Rituals to attract wealth and financial success
- Manifesting unexpected money and financial windfalls
- Prosperity spells for long-term financial stability

These are the foundational rituals my followers love and return to. Using everyday tools like bay leaves, cinnamon, and visualization, you'll call in abundance with ease.

These rituals are simple, powerful, and designed to shift your money energy fast.

Ritual 1: Bay Leaf Ritual for Manifesting Money

Materials:
- Bay leaf (one whole, dry)
- Sharpie (black or green)
- Matches or a candle (white or money-colored)
- Tweezers
- Fireproof container

Day of the week: Thursday or Sunday

Moon Phase: New Moon, Waxing Moon or Full Moon

Instructions:

- In a quiet space, close your eyes and envision the exact sum of money you desire. Feel the abundance as if it's already yours.
- Using the sharpie, write the desired amount and your name on the bay leaf. You can add symbols like the money rune or dollar signs for extra empowerment.
- Hold the bay leaf with the tweezers and speak your intention aloud.

Example:

"Money flows to me in expected and unexpected ways on a continuous basis for the best of all involved. Thank you Universe. Thank you."

- Place the bay leaf in the flame—either directly in the candle's fire or inside the fireproof container and then ignite it. Allow it to burn completely.
- Once the bay leaf has burned, go outside and blow the ashes out to the universe.

Additional Notes:
- Use a white or money-colored candle for optimal energy.

Ritual 2: Blow Cinnamon in Home 1st Day of Month

Material:
1 teaspoon of cinnamon

Best day: 1st day of the month. Alternative 1st-3rd day of any month. Powerful on the 1st day or week of the year (January)

Instructions:
- On the 1st day of the month (or within the first 3 days), take a teaspoon of cinnamon.
- Hold the cinnamon in your hand. You can use your dominant (receiving) hand or your non-dominant hand (because you're sending abundance in the home).
- Go to the door of your home. This is the door to your living space. (Front door of house, apartment or room). Go outside of door and face the open door.

Say aloud:

"As I blow this cinnamon in my home, abundance comes to me now.

As I blow this cinnamon in my home, abundance comes to me now.

Money comes to me in expected and unexpected ways for the good of all involved."

- Now blow the cinnamon into your home.
- Leave it for one day. Then, sweep it up or leave it as it is. Because you used a small amount you will not see it.

Warning: Be careful of your floors or carpet.

Ritual 3: Cinnamon Hand Wash Money Ritual

Materials:
1 teaspoon of cinnamon
A Sink with running water

Best Day: 1st day of the month or Thursday/Sunday
Best Moon Phase: New or Waxing Moon

Instructions:
- Wet your hands with water.
- Sprinkle a teaspoon of cinnamon onto your wet hands and lather them up.

As you wash, say:

"As I wash my hands in cinnamon, abundance comes to me in expected and unexpected ways for the best of all involved. As I wash my hands in cinnamon, money comes to me on a continuous basis in large sums, and I thank you, and so it is!"

- Rinse your hands lightly and pat them dry.
- Keep the scent of cinnamon on your hands for the day.

Wallet Money Rituals
"My wallet is a magnet for wealth."

Ritual 1: Pyrite in Wallet Ritual

Materials:
Pyrite crystal

Instructions:
Place the pyrite crystal in your wallet or purse.
Put it next to your money for extra energy.
Set your intent by praying over the pyrite for abundance before placing it in your wallet.

———————————•◆• — •◆•———————————

Ritual 2: Bay Leaf Wallet Ritual

Materials:
Bay leaf (dry)

Instructions:
Write the amount of money desired on a bay leaf and set the intent by speaking or visualizing having it. Place the bay leaf in your wallet next to your money or dollar bills and leave it there. Once it crumbles, replace it.

Ritual 3: High John Root in Wallet

Materials:
High John Root

Instructions:
Place a small High John Root in your wallet near your money. Set your intention for it to bring money to you. Leave it there and let go.

————————•◦— ◦•————————

Ritual 4: Basil Money Wallet Ritual

Materials:
Basil (dried or fresh)

Instructions:
Place basil in your wallet to bring in money and abundance. Always set your intent while placing it in your wallet.

————————•◦— ◦•————————

Ritual 5: Money Parchment Wallet Ritual

Materials:
A piece of parchment paper (or any paper)
Pen

Instructions:
Write your money desires on the paper.
Place the paper in your wallet.
Read it 1-3 times daily and see the money come to you.

Ritual 6: Cinnamon Dollar Bill Ritual

Material:
Paper money (Dollar bill or higher)
Tsp of cinnamon powder
Water in bowl or cup

Best: New Moon or Waxing Moon (Thursday/Sunday)
or 1st day of the month

Instructions:
- Gather items
- Wet bill in water by dipping or sprinkling
- Sprinkle cinnamon powder on bill the long way coming towards you.
- Use your finger and draw a line towards you using the cinnamon.
- Fold the wet bill with the cinnamon in half towards you.
- Turn and repeat folding towards you until small.
- Place in wallet near money or coins.
- During ritual: Say prayer or affirmation to set intent.

Ritual 7: Bill Return to Me Ritual

Materials:
Cash (bills)
Your intention

Instructions:
- Every time you spend money, hand over your bills with the face side facing you—as if watching the money come back.
- Say softly or in your mind or quietly to yourself:

"As I send this bill out, it returns to me multiplied by ten."

- This ritual reminds the Universe—and your subconscious—that money circulates, and you're always in the receiving stream.

Ritual 8: Prosperity Wallet Ritual

Materials:
Your wallet or purse
A bill (preferably high-value)

Instructions:
- Always keep your wallet or purse clean and organized.
- Place at least one bill inside—face facing you when you open it.
- Arrange your bills in order, with the highest denomination in front.
- This small action creates a feeling of wealth, sending the message:

"I always have money. I am prosperous."

Ritual 12: Lucky Hand Wallet Ritual

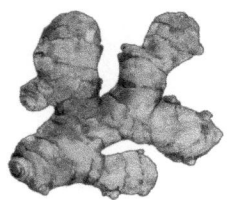

Materials:
Lucky Hand root

Instructions:
- Place a Lucky Hand Root inside your wallet or money purse.
- Keep it close to your money or change.

This powerful root is known to attract luck, and money.

Money Candle Rituals
"As this flame burns, my abundance rises."

Ritual 1: Candle Money Ritual

Materials:
Green candle (or white if needed)
Ground money herbs (cinnamon, basil, etc.)
Intention oil (money drawing, prosperity, magnet oil, or olive oil if set with intent)
Pencil
Paper towel
Florida Water

Day of the Week:
Thursday or Sunday

Moon Phase:
New Moon, Waxing Moon, or Full Moon

Steps:

Place a paper towel on your work surface. Cleanse the candle with Florida Water (or use sage or prayer).

If the candle is large, carve your name and desired amount into it. If not, write your name and amount on a small piece of parchment paper or regular paper.

Apply the intention oil to the candle. Roll it between your hands with the wick pointing toward you, to draw money to you.

Sprinkle or roll the candle in the ground money herb(s).

While anointing the candle, say:

**"As I anoint this candle,
money comes to me in expected and unexpected ways,
for the best of all involved.
This candle brings to me money and abundance.
My intention is set.
It is already done, and so it is!"**

Place the candle on a plate or in a candle holder with the paper (if used) under the plate or candle holder. Then light the candle. Sit with it until it burns out.

For a larger candle, let it burn over a couple of days until finished. Snuff it out when you leave and reignite when you come back.

Warning: Never leave a burning candle unattended. Use a candle snuffer to extinguish it—do not blow it out.

Ritual 2: Money Candle Ritual

Material:
Money candle (open road, rue candle etc.)

Instructions:
- Burn a 7-day money candle on a Thursday.
- Visualize yourself having what you desire
- Snuff out when finish for the day and reignite the next day.
- You may anoint the candle with money attracting oils
- Important to set the intention of desire.

Ritual 3: 7-Knob Money Candle Ritual

Materials:
7-knob candle (green, gold, or white)
Intention oil: Attraction, Magnet, or Money Drawing Oil
Paper and pen
Candle holder or fire-safe plate

Best Time:
Thursday or Sunday, during a New or Waxing Moon

Instructions:
- Write your money desire on a piece of paper—state it as if it's already yours.
- Place the paper under the candle holder.
- Anoint each knob of the candle with oil, rubbing upward or towards you while setting your intention.
- Light and burn one knob per day for seven days.
- Each day, as you light the next knob, say:

**"With this flame, I move closer to my goal.
Money comes to me in expected and unexpected ways.
It is done. Thank you."**

- Keep your intention strong and visualize the outcome clearly with each burn.

Pillow Money Rituals

"Even in rest, I attract prosperity."

Ritual 1: Pillow Coin Money Ritual

Materials:

One coin or your currency

Instructions:

- Hold the coin in your hand.

Say, "Money comes to me easily on a continuous basis. Thank you for it is done."

Place the coin under your pillow before you sleep and visualize the money being in your possession.

Ritual 2: Bay Leaf Money Dream Ritual

Materials:

One bay leaf (you can write your money wish on it)

Instructions:

- Write the amount you want on the bay leaf.
- Place the bay leaf under your pillow.
- Before drifting off to sleep, imagine money coming to you.
- You can also do this holding the bay leaf before placing it under your pillow.

Ritual 3: Herbal Sachet Pillow Ritual

Materials:

A small sachet or cloth bag

Dried basil (or other money herbs)

Instructions:

- Fill the sachet with the basil or other money herbs.
- Hold the sachet and say:

"I invite abundance into my life. Abundance now comes to me for the good of all involved."

- Tuck the sachet under your pillow before bed. *
- Visualize having the money desired.

Ritual 4: Money Paper Pillow Affirmation

Materials:

A small piece of paper

A pen

Instructions:

- Write your money wish on the paper. Read it 3X's
- Fold it towards you and place it under your pillow.

In the morning, read 3X's your wish and say:

"My life is now over flowing with abundance in many ways for the best of all involved."

- Know that it is already done.

Ritual 5: Write 7 Times Pillow Ritual

Materials:

- A piece of paper (or parchment)
- A pen

Instructions:

- Before bed, write your money desire 7 times on the paper.
- Read it aloud as you write each time.
- As you write, picture yourself already having the money.

- Fold the paper towards you and place it under your pillow.
- Each night for 7 days, read your wish 7 times.
- On the 7th night, finish the ritual by burning the paper, burying it, or carrying it with you until your desire is shown.

Note:
Keep calm and believe that your money is on its way.

———————————————

Ritual 6: Money Crystal Dream Ritual

Materials:
Money crystal

Instructions:
- Hold the money crystal in your hands before bed.

Set your intent:
"I call on my dreams to reveal to me the path to create money and wealth. As it is revealed to me I will take action knowing it is already done. Thank you!"

- Place the crystal under your pillow.
- For 7 days, focus on your intention as you sleep.
- After 7 days, carry the crystal in your wallet or purse, expecting the best.

Other Money Attraction Rituals

Ritual 1: Crystal Money Magick

- Carry a pyrite, green aventurine or citrine crystal with you daily to attract money and wealth.
- Clear or cleanse it prior to use by saying a prayer, sage it or set it out in the moonlight.

Then program it before carrying it for money and wealth by saying:

" I now program this crystal to assist me in attracting abundance in all forms for the best of all involved and so it is"

Ritual 2: Candle Money Magick

- Burn a green candle or another money colored candle for 7 days and visualized what you want as you sit with it.
- If possible carve your name and desire in the candle before burning.

Ritual 3: Fehu Rune Wealth Ritual

Materials:
Image or draw the Fehu rune sign (ᚠ)
Green candle
Pen or marker
Paper or parchment

Best Time:
Thursday or Sunday, New or Waxing Moon

Instructions:
- Draw or print the Fehu rune (ᚠ) on a piece of paper.
- Below it, write a short intention like:

"I attract wealth and opportunity with ease. Thank you."
- Place the paper in front of a green candle.
- Light the candle and say:

"Universe open the doors of abundance. I receive all with grace. My wealth flows freely."

- Focus on the rune glowing in your mind as the candle burns.
- Keep the paper in your wallet, money altar, or under a prosperity bowl.

Money Scripting Rituals
"I write it. I believe it. I receive it."

Scripting is writing your desires as if they've already happened. It programs your mind to believe, feel, and attract what you want. Here are powerful and simple scripting methods to bring more money into your life:

Ritual 1: "It Works" Scripting Technique:

Materials:

Paper or parchment paper

Pen or pencil

Best: Any time. Great during new moon, waxing moon or Thursday/Friday

Instructions:

- Write your money or wealth desires in order of importance.
- Be clear but keep short
- Read it 3 x daily.
- Expect the best and know that your desire is manifesting now.
- Be grateful for what the Universe has already given you, knowing that those that are grateful get more.
- Release and let go!
- Best done if consistent for 28 days.
- It's ok to change the order or the list. Just start over.

Ritual 2: "369" Scripting Technique

Material:
Paper, Parchment paper or Journal
Pen or pencil

Best: New Moon or Waxing Moon (Thursday or Saturday)

Instructions:
- Know what you want.
- Write a statement of your desire as if you already have it. Like: "I am so grateful to now have $50,000"
- Make sure the statement is clear about your desires
- Write the statement 3 times a day (morning, noon and night before bed.) Like: 9am, 3pm and 9pm
- Choose times good for you.
- Repeat for 28 days
- Let go of the who, when and how
- Take action (play lotto, apply for a grant etc.)
- Belief and confidence will get you there at a blink of an eye!

Ritual 3: The 100x Scripting Method

Materials:

Paper or notebook

Pen

Instructions:

- Write Your Statement: Choose a short, powerful money affirmation.
  (Example: "Money comes to me easily and often.")

- Write It 100 Times in One Sitting:
- As you write, visualize having the money. Feel & Believe It.
      Stay in the energy of "it is already done."
- After writing, you may:
1. Burn it to release your desire to the universe
2. Carry it in your wallet or purse and read it daily for continued focus
- Trust the Process:
- Let go of the "how." The universe will reveal the way in divine timing. Your only job is to hold the energy and believe.
- Take wise action as you feel to do so!

×55

Writing your statement 55 times is known as the 55x Method, a powerful technique rooted in the energy of change. The number 5 carries the vibration of movement, breakthrough, and transformation.

Ritual 4: The 55x Method

Materials:
Paper or notebook
Pen

Instructions:
- Choose a Short Affirmation:
        Example:
    "Money flows to me with ease."

- Write your affirmation 55 times each day for 5 days in a row.
- As you write, visualize yourself already having the money and feel the joy of receiving it.
- Let Go of the "How":
    Don't worry about how it will happen—trust divine timing and keep your heart open.

Other Scripting Rituals

Ritual 5: . Gratitude Scripting

Materials:

Paper and pen

Instructions:
- Write what you're thankful for concerning money—no matter how small. Then write what you want, but in the present tense.
Example:
"I am so thankful that I receive money easily and that I always have more than enough."

- Do this daily to build a strong mindset of wealth and gratitude.

Ritual 6: (7 Day) Repetition Scripting

Materials:

Paper and pen

Instructions:
- Write one money affirmation 20 to 30 times a day for 7 days. Focus and feel the words as you write.
Example:
"Money flows to me in increasing amounts every day."
- Expect and know it is already done.

Ritual 7: . Narrative Scripting

Materials:
Journal or notebook

Instructions:
- Write a short story about your life as if your money goals have already happened. Use present tense and include emotion and detail.
- Re-write or read it every night before bed for 7-28 days.

Example:
"I wake up, check my account, and smile. I have more than enough to pay my bills and invest. I feel peaceful and secure."

———————————— ⋅⊰ — ⊱⋅ ————————————

Ritual 8: This or Something Better Scripting Ritual

Materials:
Paper and pen

Instructions:
- Write your exact money goal. End with the phrase:
"...or something even better."

Example:
"I earn $10,000 a month doing what I love... or something even better."
This keeps your energy open to greater possibilities.

- Re-write or read it 1-2 times daily for 28 days
- Release and let go

Career & Job Success
"The perfect opportunity is already mine."

- Rituals for job offers and new career opportunities
- Manifesting a promotion and salary increase
- Confidence and interview success spells

Whether you're manifesting a new job, a raise, or more confidence at work, this section is your go-to. These rituals are designed to support interviews, promotions, and career clarity with spiritual power behind you.

Ritual 1: Job Offer Candle Ritual

Materials:
Green or yellow candle
Paper and pen
Attraction oil (or olive oil programmed for career success)

Best Time:
Thursday or Sunday, Waxing or New Moon

Instructions:
- Write the name of the company or the job title you desire on the paper.
- Anoint the candle and say:

"I am the perfect fit. The offer comes now. It is mine."

- Light the candle and visualize the offer being emailed, called in or given in person.
- Burn the candle daily until the job arrives.

Ritual 2: Confidence Before the Interview (Tiger's Eye Wear)

Materials:
Tiger's eye stone or bracelet
Best Time:
Before a job interview, presentation, or review

Instructions:
- Hold or wear tiger's eye and say:

"I am calm, clear, and confident. My energy speaks success."

- Let the stone absorb nervous energy and reflect strength.

Ritual 3: Business Card Manifestation

Materials:
- Blank card or old business card
- Pen

Best Time: Anytime

Instructions:
- Create a "future you" business card.
- Write your name, title, and dream job/company.
- Keep it in your wallet, on your altar, or near your vision board.
- This is card holds the energy of your desire..

Ritual 4: Bay Leaf Promotion Boost

Materials:
Bay leaf
Pen
Lighter or candle
Fireproof dish

Best Time: New or Waxing Moon

Instructions:
- Write your name and the title you want (e.g., "Manager," "Director") on the bay leaf.

Say:
"I now step into my new role. I rise with ease."

- Burn the leaf and release the energy. Blow the ashes out to the Universe and expect the best.

Ritual 5: Scripting for Salary Increase

Materials:
Journal or paper
Pen

Best Time: 7 days in a row

Instructions:
- Write this sentence 7 times each day:
  "I am so grateful that my salary has increased to $_____."

- Visualize your paycheck or direct deposit as you write.
- Believe it's already done.
- Keep the paper or burn it on the final day under a white or green candle.

Ritual 6: Visualization for Career Alignment

Materials: None
Best Time: Morning

Instructions:
- Visualize yourself walking into your dream job—happy, welcomed, respected.
- Visualize your desk, your workspace, your coworkers congratulating you.

Say: "I belong here. I am aligned with my perfect career."

- Know it's already done and take action when needed.

————————•◆▷—◁◆•————————

Ritual 7: Morning Affirmation for Career Growth

Materials: Your voice
Best Time: Each morning

Instructions:
- Speak this out loud:

"I am seen, valued, and rewarded in my work. Every day brings me closer to my next level."

- Expect the best and take action every day.

Bonus: Carry a Tiger's Eye, Black Tourmaline or Carnelian Crystal daily.

Ritual 8: Green Aventurine Bracelet for Career Flow

Materials: Green aventurine, pyrite, tiger's eye or black tourmaline bracelet

Best Time: Every day

Instructions:
- Wear green aventurine (or another prosperity bracelet of your choosing) to attract opportunities and smooth transitions.
- Before wearing it, hold it and say:

"I am open to new career opportunities. Prosperity follows me now."

Ritual 9: Candle Magick for Career Success

Material:
Success colored candle: Orange, Red, Green or White

Intention Oil for Success at work: Success oil, High John Oil, Road Opener Oil, or any other oil of your choosing.

Best time: Sunday, Thursday. New, Waxing or Full Moon.

Instructions:
- Carve your desire into the candle, if large enough. If not: Write your desire on paper or parchment paper in the present tense as if you already have it.
- Anoint the candle with the oil or oils of your choice applying it towards you with the wick facing you.
As you anoint it, state:

As I set my intention in the is candle, I am setting the energy in motion for my desire (-------) to manifest now. Thank you Universe. It is done!"

- Light the candle and let it burn until completed. If a large candle, snuff it out and relight the next day making the same statement.
- Do for 7 days and let it go, knowing it is already done.

———————————————•◆▷ — ◁◆•———————————————

Ritual 10: Color Magick for Success

Material:
Black, Red, White, Orange Clothes

Best Time: Every time

Instructions:
- When you want to make an impression at work wear power colors.
- Wear all black for power. Orange for success. White to stand out and Red for boldness.

Business Success
"My business thrives with purpose and profit."

- Attracting clients and business success
- Manifesting funding, loans, and business expansion
- Prosperity rituals for entrepreneurs

Whether you're running a business, offering a service, or building a brand, this section is for you. These rituals will help you attract clients, increase income, and expand with confidence.

Using simple tools like candles, crystals, affirmations, and sacred symbols, you'll align your business with steady success and spiritual flow.

Ritual 1: Money Bowl by the Door Ritual

Materials: (Money and success attracting)
Small decorative dish or bowl
Bay leaves
Cinnamon sticks or ground cinnamon
Whole nutmeg
Green aventurine
Pyrite (fool's gold)

Best Time:
 Set it up on a Thursday or Sunday
 Bless it daily

Instructions:
- Create a beautiful money bowl to place by the front door of your business or workspace.
- In the bowl, arrange the bay leaves, cinnamon, nutmeg, green aventurine, and pyrite in a way that looks natural and decorative.
- Each time you pass it, say:

"My business is blessed. Money flows in. Clients come with ease. Abundance surrounds this space."

- Keep the bowl clean and refreshed as needed.
- This bowl is a powerful magnet—blessing your space without saying a word.

Ritual 2: High John or Road Opener Candle Ritual for Business Blessings

Materials:
High John candle and/or Road Opener candle
Business name
Prosperity, Success or Business oil (Olive oil alternative)

Best Time:
Thursday, Sunday, or New/Waxing Moon

Instructions:
- Cleanse the candle(s)
- Dress with oil with wick facing you. If in jar on top of jar candle.
- Place your business name or goal under the candle if in jar or under candle holder.
- Light the candle(s) and say:

"I open the road to my success. My business is blessed, my path is clear, and I welcome growth."
or say **" High John conqueror this"**

- Let burn safely or in sessions.

Ritual 3: Prosperity Business Bath (Herbal)

Materials:
Basil, cinnamon, bay leaves, mint
White or green candle
Bowl or pot to boil herbs

Instructions:
- Boil herbs and strain.
- Pour into your bath or over your body in the shower.

As you pour, say:

"I cleanse myself of scarcity and align with success. My business blooms now."

- Let air dry and light a candle after to seal the work.

————————•◦❖ — ❖◦•————————

Ritual 4: Crystal Power for Entrepreneurs

Material: Money crystal of choice

- Wear or carry one of the following:
- Carnelian – confidence and creativity
- Tiger's Eye – protection and decision-making
- Pyrite – business attraction and money magnet
- Clear Quartz – clarity and amplification
- Citrine – cash flow and optimism

Say:

"With this crystal, I carry success energy into my day."

Ritual 5: Blow Cinnamon at Your Business Door

Materials:
Teaspoon of cinnamon

Instructions:
- Stand outside your business door (or home office if online).

Say:

"As I blow this cinnamon in, abundance flows in. Clients come, money comes, success grows."

- Blow the cinnamon into the space and leave it for the day.

Ritual 6: Scripting Business Growth

Materials:
Journal or paper
Pen

Instructions:
- Write:

"I am so thankful that my business is thriving. Clients come with ease. My income grows every day."

- Write it 7 times daily for 7 days.
- Keep the paper near your workspace or in your cash drawer.

Ritual 7: Sacred Symbols for Business Manifestation

Material:
Sri Yantra or Metatron's Cube or Tree of Life (pendant, statue, picture etc.)
Instructions:
- Place one of the symbols near your register, office, or on your vision board:
1. Sri Yantra – prosperity and expansion
2. Metatron's Cube – divine order and flow
3. Tree of Life – long-term growth

- Place it somewhere visible and say:

"This symbol activates abundance and aligns my business with divine flow."

Ritual 8: Elephant for Prosperity

Materials:
Small elephant statue (trunk up)

Instructions:
- Place near the entrance of your business facing inward.
- This invites wealth and wisdom in.
Say:

"With strength, power, and grace, success enters this space."

Ritual 9: Business Entrance Affirmation

Materials: Your voice
Best time: Start of the day when you enter your business.

Instructions:
- Each time you open your business or start your work day, say:
  "Today, my business receives an abundance of clients, money, and miracles."
- This creates a ritual of confidence and invitation.

Ritual 10: The Congratulations Technique (Visualization)

Material: Your thoughts
Best time: Any time

Instructions:
- Close your eyes and picture staff/partners or friends/family congratulating you for your business success and prosperity
- Hear:
  "I'm so proud of you! You did it! Congratulations"
- Visualize invoices being paid, orders coming in, and joyful success around you.
- Do daily or weekly.

Ritual 11: Cash Drawer Ritual

Materials:
Bloodstone, Citrine or Jade
A $1 bill
Bay leaf with "Success" written on it

Instructions:
- Place these items in your cash drawer or money box.

Say:

"This drawer attracts wealth. Every dollar multiplies."

- Keep it organized and don't spend the bill—it holds the energy of overflow.

Manifest a Home & Car
"I am aligned with the perfect place and ride."

- Rituals for getting approved for a mortgage or rental
- Attracting the perfect home
- Blessing and protecting a new home for prosperity
- Rituals for buying or leasing a car
- Attracting auto financing and finding the right deal

This section is for manifesting the big things—a home, a car, or anything physical that brings comfort, stability, and joy.

You'll find rituals using color photos, scripting, bay leaves, candles, oils, and real-life visits to create the feeling of "It's already mine."

Ritual 1: Picture It & Claim It Ritual

Materials:
A printed color photo of the house, car, or item you desire.
Red or yellow marker or pen
Tape or magnet

Best Time:
Anytime, especially during the New or Waxing Moon

Instructions:
- Print a clear, color photo of what you desire—your dream home, car, or other goal.
- Across the image, write in bold letters:
  ### "THANK YOU."
  or
  ### "Thank you, Universe—It's Done!"
- Use bright, high-vibration colors like red or yellow for energy and attraction.
- Place the photo somewhere you'll see it often: on your fridge, bathroom mirror, desk, or car visor.
- Each time you look at it, smile and feel like it's already yours.
- Say out loud or silently:
  ### "Thank you—it's done."
- Take action by putting in applications, going to the dealer. The Universe will let you know when it is right to move forward.

Ritual 2: Script Your Desire Into Reality

Materials:
Notebook, journal, or parchment paper
Pen

Best Time: Anytime, especially during the New or Waxing Moon

Instructions:
- Write out your desire as if it's already done.
- Be specific and speak with gratitude. For example:
"Thank you, God. I now have my 3-bedroom, 3-bathroom home in the perfect neighborhood for the perfect price."*
- Read what you wrote 1 to 3 times daily.
- As you read, close your eyes and visualize yourself living in the space or driving the car.
- Feel the peace, excitement, and joy as if it's already yours.
- Keep the page somewhere private or carry it with you until it manifests.
- This ritual aligns your spirit with the outcome—and the universe responds.
- Take wise action, but have fun and you will find yourself in the right place at the right time.

Ritual 3: Bay Leaf Manifestation Ritual

Materials:
Bay leaf
Pen
Lighter or candle
Fireproof dish

Instructions:
- Write your desire on a bay leaf.
- Hold it in your hand and visualize already having it.
- Burn it safely and blow the ashes into the wind under a New, Waxing, or Full Moon, saying:

"Thank you Universe—it is now mine!"

Ritual 4: Visit & Feel Ritual

Materials:
None, just your presence

Instructions:
- Visit the house, car, or place connected to your goal.
- Act as if you're ready to buy. Walk through, touch it, speak to it, feel it.
- Say:

"This is mine."

- Feel it as real. That energy activates the manifestation.

Ritual 5: Candle Manifestation Ritual

Materials:
White, green, brown, or gold candle
Carving tool
Intention oil: Attraction, Magnet, High John, or Road Opener
Picture or paper with your desire

Instructions:
- Carve your name and desire into the candle.
- Anoint it with oil, rubbing toward you.
- Place a picture or written desire under or in front of the candle.
- Light the candle and say:

"With this flame, I claim what is already mine and it is done. Thank you Universe."

- Keep the paper or picture with you looking at it and visualizing your desire.
- Take action when you feel it it right.

Ritual 6: Sit & Visualize Ritual

Materials:
Quiet space or the physical location

Instructions:
- Sit in front of the actual house, car, or an image of your desire.
- Close your eyes and visualize being inside of it—driving, relaxing, living.
- Feel joy, peace, and ownership.

Say:
"Thank you—it's already mine."

Ritual 7: Door Anointing Ritual

Materials:
Intention Oil: Attraction, Magnet or Road Opener oil

Instructions:
- Stand at the door of the home or space you want.
- Place a small amount of oil on the door frame or knob and say:

"As I anoint this door, I step into ownership. This home is mine. It is done."

Ritual 8: Vision Board Ritual

Materials:
Poster or board
Pictures of your home, car, or items desired
Markers
Best time:
Anytime but best during a New Moon or
Thursday/Sunday

Instructions:
- Create a vision board with images and words that reflect what you want.
- Add **"Thank You"** and affirmations all over it.
- Look at it daily and visualize your life with those blessings.
- Feel it, believe it, and every time you see it say:
  ### "Thank you, Universe."

Ritual 9: St. Joseph Home Manifestation Ritual

Materials:
Small St. Joseph statue
Plastic wrap or zip bag (to protect it)
Small shovel or trowel

Best Time:
During a Waxing Moon or when actively pursuing the property

Instructions:
- Wrap the statue to protect it, then bury it upside down near the front of the property you desire.
- Face the statue toward the home to symbolically draw you into it.
- As you bury it, say:

"St. Joseph, I ask for your help in receiving this home.
Let the path be cleared, the blessing be granted, and all things align in divine timing.
Thank you—it is already mine."

- When possible (daily), stand near the spot and visualize yourself in the home—decorating, relaxing, smiling, and giving thanks.
- Once the home is yours, dig up the statue and place it in your new space as a sign of gratitude and honor.

Clear Money Blocks
"I release all that stands between me and wealth."

- Releasing financial fears and limiting beliefs
- Cord-cutting for financial trauma
- Debt-banishing and clearing negative money energy

Before money can flow in, we must clear what's blocking it. This section includes natural rituals to release fear, doubt, lack, or stagnant energy.
Using tools like salt, herbs, sage, and intention, you'll create space for prosperity to enter.

Ritual 1: Money Herbal Boil

Materials:
Cinnamon sticks or ground cinnamon
Basil (fresh or dried)
Bay leaves
Pot of water
Stove or heat source
Long-handled spoon

Best Time:
1st of the month
Beginning of the year
Thursday or Sunday
New Moon or Waxing Moon

Ritual 3: Sea Salt Wallet Cleanse Ritual

Materials:

A pinch of sea salt

Instructions:

Sprinkle a very small amount of sea salt in your wallet. This will clear away bad energy and attract abundance.

Ritual 4: Sage Home

Materials:

Sage (bundle, stick or loose)

Incense burner or plate

Instructions:

- Gather material and burn sage (make sure it is smothering. You only need the smoke.
- Starting from front door of house, apartment or room.
- Walk clockwise around home.
- Sage up and down windows and doors to clear energy.
- Bonus: Follow ritual burning cinnamon to bring in abundance.

Ritual 5: Sea Salt Bath

Materials:
2-3 Tbsp of sea salt
Tub or shower

Instructions:
- Take a sea salt bath by sprinkling water on yourself while in tub.
- If not tub, use a bucket to pour over self in shower.

Ritual 6: Cinnamon + Salt Floor Sweep

Materials:
- Ground cinnamon
- Sea salt
- Broom and dustpan

Instructions:
- Mix a bit of cinnamon with sea salt and sprinkle it lightly across your floors.

As you sweep, say:

"I clear this space of lack and open the way for wealth to enter."

- Sweep it all toward the front door and discard it outside or in outside garbage.
- Good after financial arguments, money stress, or lower financial energy in the home.

Ritual 7: Lemon & Bay Leaf Boil (Block Breaker)

Materials:
Sliced lemon
Bay leaves
Pot of water

Instructions:

- Boil lemon slices and bay leaves to release cleansing energy into your space.
- Walk through your home with the steam, saying:

"All blocks to wealth are gone. Only abundance remains."

Lemon clears negativity: bay leaf welcomes prosperity.

Ritual 8: Burn & Release Block Ritual

Materials:
Small piece of paper
Pen
Fireproof container or dish
Match or candle

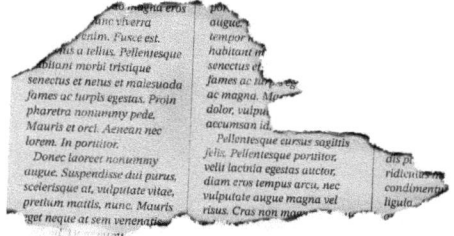

Instructions:
- Write down any beliefs or habits you feel block your money (e.g., "I don't deserve money," or "It's hard to keep money").
- Burn the paper and say:

"I release all blocks to money now. I am open, I am worthy, I receive."

- Blow the ashes outside.

Ritual 9: Spiritual Floor Wash with Florida Water

Materials:
- Florida Water
- A bucket of warm water
- A splash of vinegar (optional)
- Mop or cloth

Instructions:
- Mix a capful of Florida Water into the water and mop your floors—starting from the back of the house to the front door.

Say aloud:

"I remove all spiritual clutter and open the way for abundance."

This clears old energy from the ground up—literally.

Ritual 10: Salt and Vinegar Debt Clearing Bath
(When you are in debt)

Materials:
Sea salt (If no allergies)
Apple cider vinegar (If no allergies)
White candle

Best Time: Saturday, Waning Moon

Instructions:
- Draw a warm bath and add a handful of sea salt and a cup of apple cider vinegar.
- Light the white candle and focus on cleansing yourself of the negative energy associated with unpaid debts.
- Soak for at least 15 minutes, visualizing the debt dissolving away.
- After the bath, allow yourself to air dry.

———————— •◈ — ◈• ————————

Ritual 11: Visualize Debt Repayment
Material:
Your Imagination

Best Time: Before bed or early morning

- Image the debtor paying you back or receiving the money.
- Be creative, knowing the debt is paid in full.

Ritual 12: Candle Banishing Debt Ritual

Materials:
Black or White candle
Piece of paper
Black pen
Fireproof dish

Best Time: Saturday, Waning Moon

Instructions:
- Write the debt and debtor's name on the piece of paper.
- Anoint the black candle with banishing oil if available.
- Light the candle and focus on removing the obstacle of unpaid debt.

Say:
"I release this debt from my life; it no longer holds power over me."

- Burn the paper in the fireproof dish using the candle flame.
- Let the candle burn down safely.

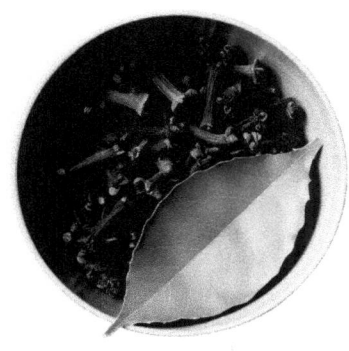

Ritual 13. Burn Clove & Bay Leaf (Light Smoke Cleanse)

Materials:

A few cloves

One bay leaf

Charcoal disk or small fire-safe burner

Instructions:

- Burn clove and bay leaf together (on charcoal if needed) and allow the smoke to gently fill your space.

Say:

"I dissolve all lack, I welcome flow. Abundance, come forth now."

Clove is fiery and strong—great for breaking stuck energy.

Win Money & Financial Rewards
"Unexpected blessings flow to me now."

- Winning lottery or good fortune at the casino
- Getting approved for financial aid, grants, and funding

This section is all about aligning with luck, unexpected income, and financial blessings.
Perfect for lottery wins, games of chance, or surprise breakthroughs—these rituals tap into the frequency of fortune.

Ritual 1: Nutmeg Luck Booster

Materials:
Whole nutmeg

Instructions:
- Place a whole nutmeg in your wallet or purse.
- Before playing the lottery or going to the casino, hold it in your hand and set your intention.

Say:

"Nutmeg, bring fortune and luck to me. May money flow in expected and unexpected ways."

- Keep it with you when playing or entering places of chance.

Tip: Nutmeg is known for bringing luck in gambling and quick cash.

Ritual 2: Bay Leaf Gambling Wish

Materials:
- Bay leaf
- Pen or sharpie
- Fireproof container
- Candle or lighter

Instructions:
- Write your wish on the bay leaf: "Win the lottery," "Big casino win," or your lucky numbers.

- Burn the bay leaf in a candle flame or fireproof container.

Say:

"This wish is sealed. Luck surrounds me. I win now."

- Blow the ashes outside.

Ritual 3: Money Candle Luck Ritual

Materials:
- Green, gold, or white candle
- Money oil (or olive oil programmed for money)
- Small piece of paper
- Pen

Best Time: Thursday or Sunday, New or Waxing Moon.

Instructions:
- Anoint the candle with money oil, rolling on the candle towards you.
- Write your desire on the paper and place it under the candle holder.
- Light the candle and say:

"Luck and success flow to me now. I receive unexpected money with joy and ease."

- Let the candle burn completely or snuff it out and relight daily until finished.
- Do not leave a burning candle unattended.

Ritual 4: Cinnamon & Sugar Hand Wash

Materials:

Small bowl of warm water

Cinnamon (a pinch)

Sugar (a pinch)

Instructions:

- Add cinnamon and sugar to warm water.
- Wash your hands with it before playing or going to a casino.

  Say: **"As I sweeten my hands, I sweeten my luck. Good fortune comes easily to me now."**

- Pat dry and feel the energy on your hands.

———————————— •◈› — ‹◈• ————————————

Ritual 5: Lucky Sachet Bag

Materials:

Small green pouch or cloth

Nutmeg

Bay leaf

Clear quartz or lodestone

Cinnamon (a pinch)

Instructions:

- Place all items in the pouch.
- Hold it in your hand and set the intention for luck and big wins.

  Say: **"Luck flows. Money comes. I receive it with ease."**

- Carry it with you when playing games of chance.

Ritual 6: Grant & Financial Support Ritual

Materials:
Piece of paper
Green or gold pen
Bay leaf
White candle
Money oil or olive oil (programmed)

Best Time:
Thursday or Sunday, New Moon or Waxing Moon.

Instructions:
- Write the type of financial support you need on the paper (example: "$5,000 scholarship," or "Grant approved for my business").
- Anoint the candle and set your intention.
Say:
"I receive this funding now. The right people say yes. The way is open."
- Place the bay leaf on top of the paper and light the candle.
- Visualize the approval coming through.
- Burn the bay leaf before the candle finishes or carry it with the paper until the money comes.

95

Ritual 7: Lottery Candle Blessing Ritual

Materials:
Lottery ticket
Green or gold candle
Gambling Oil, Attraction Oil, or Magnet Oil (or a programmed olive oil)
Fire-safe plate or holder

Best Time:
Thursday or Sunday
New or Waxing Moon

Instructions:

- Anoint your candle with the oil, rubbing it upward or towards you while focusing on the outcome.
- Place your lottery ticket near or under the candle holder but where it won't get harmed.
- Light the candle and say the following prayer:

Prayer:
"Universe, align me with divine luck.
Let this ticket carry the vibration of abundance.
If it is in my highest good, may it bring fortune my way. I release and trust that blessings are already mine. Thank you, thank you, thank you."

- Let the candle burn safely each day before the drawing.

Pay Me My Money
"What is owed to me returns multiplied."

- Winning legal cases and financial disputes
- Receiving money this is owed to you (refunds, settlements, loans)
- From those that just don't want to pay you back!

This section is about one thing: receiving the money that is owed to you. Whether it's from a person, a company, or a past situation, these rituals are designed to call it back, and help you get paid—in full.

Ritual 1: Write it 7 Times to Be Repaid

Materials:
Paper or journal
Pen

Best Time:
New or Waxing Moon, or anytime

Instructions:
- Write the following sentence 7 times each night for 7 days:

"I am so thankful that [name or situation] has paid me in full."

- Visualize the repayment happening as you write.
- Keep the paper with you, or place it under your pillow or in your wallet until you receive the money.

Ritual 2: Visualize It Returning Now

Materials:
- Quiet space
- A few minutes of focus

Best Time:
Before bed or during meditation

Instructions:
- Sit quietly and picture yourself checking your bank account and seeing the deposit.
- Visualize receiving a text, email, or call from the person who owes you—saying:

"I've sent you the money."

- Smile. Feel the joy, the relief, the confirmation.
- Do this for just 2–3 minutes daily.

Ritual 3: Crystals to Carry for Debt Repayment

Material:
A Money crystal (Green Aventurine, Lodestone, Jade, etc.)
Attraction Oil or any money drawing oil

Instructions:
- Anoint the money crystal with attraction oil or money drawing oil.
- Set the intention in the crystal by holding it in your receiving hand and stating:

" All that is owed to me now finds it's way back to me for the best of all involved. It is now done! Thank you Universe."

- Carry the crystal in your wallet or purse until debt is repaid.

Ritual 4: Speak Your Money Back Affirmation

Materials:
Your voice and belief
Best Time:
 Every morning or night

Instructions:

- Stand in front of a mirror and speak this declaration out loud:

"I am calling in what is rightfully mine. The money that's owed to me is on its way. I am ready, I am open, I receive."

- Feel it as the truth. Look yourself in the eyes. Smile like it's already done.
- Repeat daily until the money arrives in full.

Ritual 5: Pay Me My Money Candle Ritual

Materials:
Green or gold candle
Money oil (or olive oil programmed for money)
Paper and pen
Candle Holder

Best Time:
Thursday or Sunday, New or Waxing Moon

Instructions:
- Write the name of the person, business, or situation that owes you money on a piece of paper.
- Be clear about the amount or intention.
- Anoint the candle with oil, rubbing it toward you.
- Place the paper beneath the candle holder and say:

"The money that is owed to me comes now. Paid in full, without delay. I receive it with ease."

- Light the candle and visualize the money reaching you.
- Allow it to burn out or relight each day until complete.
- Keep the paper on you until resolved.
- Alternative: Burn the paper in the candle before it burns out.

Ritual 6: Court Case Money Ritual

Materials:
Blue candle (or white if blue is unavailable)
Just Judge oil or Court Case oil (or olive oil programmed for justice)
Piece of paper
Pen
Candle holder
High John the Conqueror root (optional)

Best Time:
 Start before or during the court case.
 Best days: Thursday for money or Sunday for success

Instructions:
- Write the names of the judge, opposing attorney, and the person or company that owes you on a piece of paper.
- If the candle is large enough, carve the names directly into the wax.
- Anoint the candle with the oil, rubbing toward you to draw justice in your favor.

- Place the paper under the candle holder and light the candle.

As it burns, say:

"Justice is mine. The truth is clear. What is owed to me returns now. Thank you Universe. I win in peace and favor."

- Burn the candle daily for 7 days or until your case is resolved.
- If the candle burns for a long time, snuff it out—do not blow it out and relight when you are with it. (Don't leave a burning candle alone.

Optional: Carry a High John Root in your pocket on court day to boost courage, strength, and favor in your case.

Ritual 7: Honey Jar Ritual for Debt Repayment

Materials:
Small jar with lid
Honey
Piece of paper
Pen
Pink candle

Best Time: Friday, Waxing Moon

Instructions:
- Write the debtor's name on the piece of paper three times.
- Rotate the paper 90 degrees and write your name over theirs three times, creating a crosshatch.
- Place the paper in the jar and cover it with honey.
- Seal the jar.
- Light the pink candle in front or near the jar, focusing on sweetening the debtor's attitude toward repaying you.
- Burn a pink candle for seven consecutive days, allowing the candle to burn safely each time.
- If you are using a larger candle or 7-day candle, snuff out then relight daily for 7 days when you are in it's presence.

Ritual 8: Lodestone Attraction Ritual

Materials:
Lodestone (small piece)
Green cloth or pouch
Small paper and pen

Best Time:
Thursday or Sunday, Waxing Moon

Instructions:
- Hold the lodestone in your hands and set the intention to receive the money that is owed to you.
- Write the name of the person or situation and the amount you expect to receive on the small paper.
- Place the paper and the lodestone inside a green pouch.

Say:
"This lodestone pulls what is mine. The money owed comes now, on time."

- Carry the pouch with you or place it near your front door or cash drawer.
- Re-energize the lodestone weekly by holding it and repeating your affirmation.

Long-Term Wealth & Security
"My abundance is stable, growing, and protected."

- Generational wealth-building rituals
- Protecting finances from negative energy or loss
- Attracting multiple income sources and lasting prosperity

This section is about building and protecting wealth that lasts. These rituals help you create financial stability, attract multiple income sources, and protect what's yours from spiritual or energetic interference.

Use these everyday practices to stay aligned with abundance for the long run.

Ritual 1: Morning Alignment Affirmation

Materials: Your voice
Best Time: Every morning

Instructions:

Say aloud:
"I am building wealth with grace and ease. I am aligned with divine prosperity and lasting success."

- Speak it before checking your phone or starting your day.
- Feel the truth of those words before you move forward.

2. Wealth Crystal Bracelet Ritual

Materials: Green aventurine, tiger's eye, or citrine bracelet
Best Time: Daily or anytime when inspired

Instructions:
- Hold your bracelet and say:

"I am surrounded by opportunities, protected by wisdom, and guided toward success."

- Wear daily as a physical reminder of your energy and intention.

Ritual 3: Speak the 23rd Psalm for Divine Financial Security

Materials: Your voice or spiritual text
Best Time: Any day, preferably morning or night

Instructions:

- Recite the 23rd Psalm slowly, visualizing yourself walking a path of provision, safety, and peace.
- This helps call in divine protection over your finances and future.

Ritual 4: Visualization for Multiple Income Streams

Materials:
Quiet space
Best Time:
Morning or evening

Instructions:

- Visualize yourself receiving income from 2–3 different sources (clients, checks, passive income, new opportunities).
- Smile as you see yourself receiving and thriving.

Say: **"Money comes from many sources. I am open to receive."**

Ritual 5: Gratitude + Forgiveness for Wealth Flow

Materials:
Journal or your thoughts
Best Time: Evening

Instructions:
- Each night, write or say 3 things you're grateful for.

Then, say: **"All is well. I release all grudges and open myself to divine flow."**

This keeps your financial energy clean, open, and magnetized.

Ritual 6: Carry a Prosperity Token

Materials:
A $bill, a coin, or a crystal like pyrite
Best Time: Always

Instructions:
- Keep a physical symbol of wealth with you—like a $1bill (any bill) or pyrite stone.
- Touch it and say:

"I am a magnet for lasting wealth. It grows, it flows, and it stays."

- Use it as a reminder of abundance and stability.

Ritual 7: Weekly Energy Protection Ritual

Materials:

Sage, palo santo, or Florida Water

Best Time: Once a week

Instructions:
- Cleanse your home or money space (wallet, desk, etc.) with sage or Florida Water.

Say:

"I protect my wealth from all harm and loss. I invite only blessing and growth."

- Visualize a shield of light around your finances.

Ritual 8: Speak to Future Generations

Materials: None
Best Time: Whenever you feel called

Instructions:
- Take a quiet moment and say:

"I am building wealth that will bless those who come after me. My decisions today create ease and opportunity for tomorrow."

This ritual honors your role as a chain-breaker and abundance-creator.

Remember: It's your thought, beliefs and intentions that create your future. So think and speak wisely!

Ritual 9: Daily Celebration Visualization

Material:
Your imagination
A quiet space
Best Time: Morning or evening

Instructions:
- Close your eyes and take a deep breath.
- Visualize yourself and your loved ones celebrating —smiling, laughing, hugging, high-fiving.
- See yourself saying things like:

"We did it!"
"I can't believe it finally came through!"
"Everything worked out better than expected."

- Even if it's just you—picture yourself radiating joy and success.
- Feel the emotion. Soak it in. Let that celebration energy become your daily vibration.

Tip:
This daily ritual sends a powerful message to the Universe:

"I'm ready for blessings. I already feel the joy of receiving."

Ritual 10: Sesame Seed Prosperity Bowl

Materials:
Small bowl
Sesame seeds
Dollar bill
Loose change

Instructions:
- Place sesame seeds in a small bowl with a dollar and coins.
- Set it in your home's wealth corner or common area.

Say: **"This bowl draws wealth, luck, and overflow."**

- Let the bowl look pretty and remain there until you desire to change it.

Ritual 12: Citrine Crystal Wealth Corner

Materials:
Citrine crystal

Instructions:
Place a piece of citrine in the far-left corner of your home or main room (from the front door entrance).
This area is known as the wealth corner in Feng Shui.

Say: "Citrine, activate prosperity. Let abundance grow in this space."

Instructions:

- Place a piece of citrine in the far-left corner of your home or main room (from the front door entrance).
- This area is known as the wealth corner in Feng Shui.

Say:

"Citrine, activate prosperity. Let abundance grow in this space."

Ritual 13: Pecans at the Door Ritual

Materials:
Pecans (in shell)
Decorative bowl

Instructions:

- Place whole pecans in a decorative bowl near your front door.
- Do not eat them—they are there to welcome abundance and protection into your space.
- Each time you walk in, say:
  "Abundance greets me each day as I enter my home. Thank you."

Tip: You can also place this bowl in a business or office entryway to invite abundance in all forms.

Final Thoughts

This book is more than just a collection of rituals—it's a tool for alignment. When you begin to work with these simple yet powerful practices, you are not just attracting money, you are tuning your energy towards the frequency of abundance, success and happiness.

As you move through each ritual, remember: it's not about the herbs, the candles, or the paper alone. It's about your belief, your intention, and your willingness to align with the truth that abundance is already yours.

Be clear about what you desire. Be grateful for what you already have. Trust that the Universe is always listening. I am living proof that belief and expectation can move mountains—and they can do the same for you.

Stay open, stay faithful, and know that everything you need is already on its way.

With love,
Eyvette Risher
My World of Metaphysics

Ritual Notes:

Ritual Notes:

Ritual Notes:

Ritual Notes:

Ritual Notes:

Stay Connected with Eyvette Risher

Want more rituals, guidance, and tools for manifestation?

🌐 Visit My Website:
 Join my community, classes, and coaching.
www.MyWorldofMetaphysics.com

🛍️ **Shop Metaphysical Products:**
 Candles, oils, crystals & more.
www.store.myworldofmetaphysics.com

📺 **Watch Weekly Videos & Live Streams:**
 My World of Metaphysics on YouTube
YouTube.com/@MyWorldofMetaphysics

📚 **Explore My Other Books & Journals:**
- 369 Manifestation Journal
- Dream Interpretation Journal
- It Works Manifestation Journal

📱 **Follow Me on Social Media:**
Instagram: instagram.com/myworldofmetaphysics
Facebook: facebook.com/MyWorldOfMetaphysics
Pinterest: pinterest.com/Eyvette154
X (Twitter): x.com/MetaphysicsMy
TikTok: tiktok.com/@myworldofmetaphysics